Joan's Music

Learn to Write, Play, and Sing Songs

by

Joan Lowrance

Joan's Music

This book helps the beginner and the individual who just wants to play the piano or any instrument for their own pleasure, or for a school teacher, or for a Bible class, or any small group gathering. The book teaches you how to quickly write down a song, add some notes for the melody, and then add some basic chords for the accompaniment without having to formerly write the song in music sheet format.

I have written this book of Christian songs for everyone's enjoyment and to teach others what I did and learned so they, too, can be filled with the Lord's music and learn how to write their own music, sing on key, and play their music. You can use any instrument you want to play as it does not have to be a piano. When we traveled in our RV I would bring my guitar and pick out the music and sing.

ISBN: 978-0-578-66204-6

About the Author

I have always been a teacher from when my children were small and then helping them with their homework throughout their school years, to teaching business classes at different colleges and adult schools, to owning the Loan Officers Training Center with my husband and teaching and the in's and out's of mortgage banking, to our owning a real estate company, a mortgage loan company, and a loan processing company, to my teaching women's Bible studies.

In all of these colleges, schools, and businesses I was always teaching and training people giving them the opportunity to have a good job and career, and best of all, the Bible Studies, to tell people about Jesus Christ, the Son of God, and to see them receive Jesus Christ as their Lord and Savior. Have you asked Jesus to come into your heart? When you do, you will never be the same as His love will fill you up to overflowing.

And now I am teaching Joan's Women's Bible Study at joanswomensbiblestudy.com in a blog which I just finished writing and designing. I am calling it Joan's Women's Bible Study at joanswomensbiblestudy.com. Each Bible Study has one of these songs mentioned in the Study. Be sure to check it out!

I hope you enjoy this music book as much as I have enjoyed writing it.

Please spread the news with your reviews/comments and passing it on to others on your Facebook, Twitter pages, Joan's Women's Bible Study at joanswomensbiblestudy.com and other sites, so many people can learn to write, sing, and play, their music.

Check out our other books now available on Amazon.

Home Buying & Financing 101, by Mark Kovach
How to Establish Your Credit, by Mark Kovach
Making Parenting Simple Handbook, by Mark Kovach

Thank you for buying Joan's Music book.

Joan Lowrance

Table of Contents

How to Write, Sing, and Play Music

Songs and Music by Joan Lowrance and Mark Kovach

Introduction

As long as I can remember we have always had a piano in our home starting with Granny's very old piano where we taught ourselves how to play. My husband became a master by completing all of Alfred's books up to the third level and then some. Myself, I never got past Alfred's first level.

In the 90's my husband bought us a Kursweill Baby Grand Piano keyboard with all those beautiful sounds. Then in 2008 he bought us a Kwai upright with all the latest sounds which made his music even more beautiful. I can listen to his music for hours.

For myself, I fell in love with Christian songs and played most of the easy songs from the Maratha Music Praise Book. Then in 2003 in my very long two hour drives to visit my dad in the rest home I would always be singing songs. Then I started hearing songs from the Lord while driving in heavy traffic. I had to keep repeating the songs until I got to the rest home and find a raggedy piece of paper to scribble in shorthand the words to the song. Every trip for the three years that I made this drive the Lord would give me another song. My mom always new when I had a new song for dad and she would say, "Sing to dad your new song," and I did. The next three years the Lord's songs started coming so fast that there was no time to write them in sheet music format.

The Lord said to me, "Put My words into their mouths through song," and now I have done it beginning with this book!

I would sit down at the Kursweill and write the melody placing the note above each syllable of a word on whatever piece of scratch paper it was written on, some as small as 2"x4". Some of the music finally got typed. As the years went by the songs slowed down to about three or four a year which has given me time to put the songs the Lord has given me into typed format and a hand written note alpha letter would be written above each syllable.

As of 2019 I have been getting a little more professional as I have typed the songs and the music to write this book so others can follow what I did and learn so they, too, can enjoy the Lord's music and learn how to write their own music, sing on key, and play their music.

You can use any instrument you want to play as it does not have to be a piano. When we traveled in our RV I would bring my guitar and pick out the music and sing.

So Let's get started!

Music by Joan

How to Write, Sing, and Play Music

1. How to write music.

This book helps the beginner and the individual who just wants to play the piano or any instrument for their own pleasure, or for a school teacher, or for a Bible class, or any small group gathering. The book teaches you how to quickly write down a song, add some notes for the melody, and then add some basic chords for the accompaniment without having to formerly write the song in music sheet format. If you have never played an instrument, get a beginner's lesson book for the piano or keyboard for any instrument of your choice which will help you to know where the keys are for the notes you will want to play.

2. How to hear the right sound (note).

Listen to songs on the radio, CD, I-Pad, or on any recording device, and sing along with the song. Did you notice when the sounds or notes went up or down? Did you notice when the notes go up or down at the end of a line or when the song ended? Sing the song again and on a piece of paper write a line or two of the song down. Then take a pencil and write a dash line up or down above each syllable of each word. These dashed lines will help you in the beginning to know when to use a higher note or lower note on your keyboard or instrument. Practice this and it will become easy for you to hear the sounds of the songs you love. The more you sing along with the songs you listen to, the stronger your voice will become and for your ear to pick up just the right sound for each note.

3. How to hear a song and from the lyrics, write the music.

Let's try writing some notes for one of your favorite songs. It is best to use a slow song at first, especially, if you are a beginner at your keyboard. On your computer go to the internet and search for your song's lyrics. You will find some free sites to do this on the web. Then copy the lyrics and paste these into MS Word or Pages any other word processing program. Double space the lyrics and print these out. Sometimes the site includes an audio of the song which can help you hear the right sounds. You can also copy the sheet music for the song, however, you will have to pay for the music sheet.

4. How to write the music to your own songs.

Now you are ready to write the music for your first song. I usually write my songs beginning in Middle C and go up to the next octave including C, D, and E. And during the song sometimes I will go down below Middle C and include B, A, and G in my music for the song. Don't be afraid to hear the music different than someone else. If it sounds good to you, it's good! Everyone has their own style and rhythm; so don't be afraid to have your song sound different than someone else's music for the same song.

5. How to write music using letters of the alphabet.

Let's write some music to your song. Above each syllable of each word in your song, write a letter, i.e., A-, B-, C, D, E, F, G, A, B, C+, D+, E+, and if the letter is below Middle C, use a dash (-) before the letter; and if the letter is above Middle C, use a plus (+) after the letter. This is how I identify my notes; it's fast, easy and very easy to read when you are playing your song. Warning: When writing music, it takes a lot of time in the beginning. However, as you write more music, it will go much faster, and then you will surprise yourself when you have completed the music in one sitting. In the beginning I was lucky to complete three lines in one sitting. So don't give up. You just may have a #1 song and get a great recording contract.

6. How to use the keyboard.

A piano keyboard is a great instrument; it has many accompaniments to choose from that will blend nicely with your music. Another reason I like the piano keyboard is the fact that I can play my own personal (left hand) accompaniment along with the melody (right hand) all at the same time. You can buy a keyboard for a little as $100 at the various music stores. So you don't have to have a lot of money to make beautiful music. When I am doing a small group Bible Study, I can take my inexpensive keyboard along with me and I can play some praise music for the all of us to sing. It's great fun. I shocked my Mom and Dad one day, who did not know I could play. I walked into their home with my little keyboard and played and sang the songs I had written.   They wanted to know how I learned that and said, we didn't know you could sing. Well, I couldn't sing or play an instrument in the beginning, but as I said earlier, whenever a song is being played, just sing or hum along with it and your voice will stay in tune and it will grow stronger each time.

7. Words have music.

Often when I am listening to a program, there will be something that sings out to me as the speaker's words and voice bring music to their words to my ears. For instance, a friend of mine was reading some of her poems that she had written and as she was reading a poem, I heard the music to many of the lines of poetry. I told her some of her poetry sounds like a beautiful song could be written using your poems. She got very excited about the idea of writing a song, however, she said, she can't sing and she does not know how to play an instrument. I told her I could show her how and we set a date to meet the following week so I could show her how to write, play and sing the music. After the meeting, she bought her inexpensive keyboard and away she went. Next time we met, she had a song for me to listen to which was part of one of her poems and it was beautiful. Another friend read his poem he had just written for his fiancé to be who he was going to propose to and immediately the music rang in my ears. He asked me if I would put the poem to music and I did and recorded it for him to give it to his future wife. These are just a few examples of the many times that I have heard music in the words and I have put many of these words to songs and so can you.

8. Start with a slow song.

It is better to begin with a slow song as it will be easier for you to write the music. You don't want to overwhelm yourself and think, "Oh, writing is too difficult for me;" just take it slow and you will be amazed with your results and with the songs and music you will be able to write over time.

9. Hear the sounds of the words in your song.

When you speak or sing the words of your song, listen to the words, do the sounds go up or down in pitch? This will help you to choose the right notes for your song. When practicing your song, does it sound the same way you originally sang or hummed the song prior to writing it down on paper? Do you need to change some of the notes to reflect the true sounds of your song?

10. Keyboard beginners.

If you have never played a keyboard before, get a beginner's piano or keyboard instruction lesson book for the basics of keyboard locations, what fingers to use on the keys, and practice lessons.

11. Right Hand: Practice the keyboard starting with Middle C Octave.

You will need to practice scales on the keyboard. And while you are practicing the scales, also use your voice or hum along with the notes beginning with middle C to C+. You might remember the way students would practice the scales: It goes something like this using your voice: do, ray, me, fa, so, la, te, toe. Practice the scales forward and then backwards. Also, this is a good warm up to do prior to practicing your songs each day.

12. Left Hand: Practice the keyboard using the Octave below Middle C Octave. Lay your fingers on the keyboard with your thumb on Middle C and go down the scale to C- and then up the scale again.

13. Right Hand: Practice the keyboard using the Octave above Middle C Octave.

14. Both Hands: Practice (LH) Octave below Middle C and (RH) Middle C Octave.

15. Both Hands: Practice (LH) Middle C Octave and (RH) Octave above Middle C.

16. The sharps and flats (the black keys) omit until you have mastered the (white keys.)

17. Let's write a short song.

18. Listen to songs and notice when the notes (sounds) go up and down.

19. Make up your song. Hum or sing it and listen to the sounds.

20. Write the words to your song on paper double spaced using 14 font size for easy reading.

21. Go to the keyboard and play a note until you find the right sound that goes with your song.

22. Write a note for each syllable that you would play using your right hand.

23. Write the alpha letter (C, D, etc.) above each syllable of the word (use pencil or an erasable pen).

24. Play and sing the song on your keyboard (piano, etc.). How does it sound?

25. Make any changes to your notes.

26. Let's add some chords to your song using your left hand.

27. Use chords to emphasize certain words or notes for your song.

28. Example: For the chord of C (use your left hand and put your little finger on C, the 3rd finger on E, and your thumb on G) and play these together with Middle C (using your thumb on right hand).

29. In the beginning, you may want to write the chord above the note you want to emphasize. Later on you will have these all memorized.

30. List of chords.

31. You can use one finger, two fingers, or three fingers for the chord of C.

32. Hold the right pedal down while you play your song. It will blend your music.

33. Listed below are the chords I use and have memorized.

Melody (right hand)	Chord (left hand)
C	-G -E - -C
D	-G -F - -B
E	-G -E - -C
F	-A -F - -C

Melody (right hand)	Chord (left hand)
G	-G -E - -C
A	-A -F - -C
B	-B -G -D
C+	G C E
D+	D -B -F
E+	G C E

I think the songs played on a keyboard sound best when played in the sounds of "Classic Electric Piano" with the foot pedal on the right held down throughout the song. If you have just one pedal, hold it down as stated above.

The songs I have provided in this book I have underlined the words that I want to hold down the key longer in order to accentuate the word.

Now for some songs you can play by Joan Lowrance and one song by my husband Mark Kovach.

Keyboard Drill Practice

With your <u>right hand</u> begin on middle C with your thumb and sing with the notes. This will straighten your voice and help you to stay on key.

(-) keys below middle C and (+) are keys above B

Right hand

C	D	E	F	G	A	B	C+	D+	E+	F+	C+
Do	Re	Mi	Fa	So	La	Ti	Do				

Left hand

-G	-G	-G	-A	-G	-A	-B	G	D	G	-A	-G
-E	-F	-E	-F	-E	-F	-G	E	-B	E	-F	-E
-C	- -B	-C	-C	-C	-C	-D	C	-F	C	-C	-C

Once you have mastered the right hand forward and backwards then add the left hand with the chords as shown above again doing them forward and backwards and remember to sing.

I like to hold down the right pedal as I play as it blends the notes nicely together. I use Classic Electric Piano for all my music.

A little note: Everyone has a voice and it is through practice like this that you will always sing on key. One day my mother said to me, I didn't know you could sing. And she was right. But once I started singing with my Keyboard Drill, I was singing on key.

Psalm 150:3-6

Praise Him with the sound of a trumpet; Praise Him with the flute and harp! Praise Him with stringed instruments and flutes! Praise Him with loud cymbals, Praise Him with clashing cymbals! Let everything that has breath (that's you) praise the Lord. Praise the Lord!

The Steps of a Good Man

Psalm 37:23,24,27,29

Song & Music by Joan Lowrance - 3/17/16

```
   C   E   G  C+  B   G   C   E  G    C+  B   A
The steps of a good man are ordered by the Lord,
```

```
   C   E   G C+   B   A   G
and He delights in his way.
```

```
    C      -A  -B  -A  -B  -G  -A  -B-A-G  -B   C
Though he fall, he shall not be utterly cast down,
```

```
C    D   E   G A    G    G   A   F
For the Lord upholds him with His hand.
```

```
 C E    D   EC  C   E   G
Depart from evil and do good,
```

```
  C   E    A  G    A  BC+D+  E+   C+
(For the righteous shall inherit the land,
```

```
 C+   E+   C+  D+  C+E+C+
and dwell in it  forever.) (repeat for ending)
```

9

Worthy is the Lamb

Revelation 5:12

Song & Music by Joan Lowrance - 7/1/14

Angels, living creatures, and elders, the number of them 10,000 x 10,000
and thousands and thousands saying in a loud voice

  A F   D E C
Worthy is the <u>Lamb</u> (2)

  C   -A   -B
who was <u>slain</u>

C E G   B A   G C+ B G   B A
to receive <u>power</u> and riches and wisdom

  G   B   G   A F G   B A   G
and strength and honor and <u>glory</u> and

  C+ B   A F   D E   C
<u>blessing</u>!   Worthy is the <u>Lamb</u>.

  A F D   E C
You are so <u>worthy</u>,

  A F   D E C   E C
<u>You</u> are so worthy, <u>O Lord</u>.

God Said

2 Corinthians 6:16 & 18
Revelations 5:13
Song & Music by Joan Lowrance - 8/27/17

A F   D   E C
I will <u>dwell</u> in <u>them</u>

 C   E   D F   A
and walk among <u>them</u>.

A F D   E   C
I will be their <u>God</u>

C   E   D   F A   B G
and they shall be <u>my people</u>,

 A   F   D
<u>Says</u> the Lord.

A F D E D E   D C
I will be a <u>Father to you</u>,

 C   E   D F A   G
and you shall be my <u>sons</u>

 E   D C
and <u>daughters</u>,

 A   F   D   E   A B G
<u>Says</u> the <u>Lord God Almighty</u>.

Chorus:

C+ B   G   A F   G
<u>Blessing</u> and <u>honor</u> and

B A   G C+ B   G
<u>glory</u> and <u>power</u> be

E   C   -A   -B D   F   B
to Him who sits <u>on the throne</u>,

G   E C   A   BD+C+   A   D+C+
and to the <u>Lamb forever and ever</u>.

C+E+G+F+   CEGC
  <u>Amen</u>,   <u>Amen</u>.

Psalm 23

Song & Music by Joan Lowrance - 6/23/03

E C F A G   B C+   A B G
Let me walk in your righteous path today.

C -A -B D F   A C+ B G
Holy Spirit guide me all the way.

E   C   F   A C+   B   G A G
Let me praise the Lord and walk in His

B   D+   C+
Righteousness.   (repeat slowly for ending)

My Father Never Gives Up

Ephesians 2:4-5

Song & Music by Joan Lowrance - 3/6/13

Chorus:

G   EF   ED   E   F D E   GB
My Father never gives up on His children.

C   G E   F   GB G C+A
He welcomes them into the family,

C   A G   E   D (end in C)
The family of God.

Verse:

C   G B G
He's all loving,

C   E G E
Long suffering,

C G B A
All forgiving,

C G E   D   E   B   G
Merciful God who loves you.

(repeat chorus end in C)

Hallelujah
Praise the Lord

Song & Music by Joan Lowrance - 1/26/13

C F A G   C   D   E
Hallelujah, praise the Lord,

  C   E   A G   DE   C
Christ is coming very soon.

D F B   A   G   E   D
Hallelujah, praise the Lord,

C   E   G   A   G E   F   D
It won't be long before He's here.

C F A G   C   D   E
Hallelujah, praise the Lord,

C E   A G D   F   B   G
I love Jesus and He loves me.

D F B   A   G   E   D
Hallelujah, praise the Lord,

C   E   G   A   G E   F   D
It won't be long before He's here. (repeat line for ending)

F   B   G
He loves me. (slowly)

F   B   G
He loves me. (a little louder)

F   B   G
He loves me. (LOUDLY on keyboard and voice then repeat song)

To Be in My Father's House

John 14:1, Luke 19:38

Song & Music by Joan Lowrance - 6/21/18

D -B C E G   B A   G
O, to be in my Father's House

  D   -B   C -A -B -A -G
cause that's where I want to be

 D -B C E   G B G
singing praises to my Lord

 D -B C E   C   E A B
for giving us this wonderful

G   A B   C+
life without end.

D -B C E G   B A   G
O, to be in my Father's House

  D   -B   C E G B
where the light of the Lord

  A   B G
shines on me.

D -B C -A   E G D -B -G
O, beautiful Savior, full of love,

  C   E G F D
how great it will be

-B C -A C E   G C+
to walk in heaven with You.

Chorus:

D -B C E G D -B
Blessed is the King who comes

C -B -A -B -A -G
in the name of the Lord!

D -B C E G A B G
Peace in heaven and glory

A B D+ C+
in the highest!   (repeat slowly for ending using middle C chord)

"Give" an ear, O Heavens

Deut. 32:1-4

Song & Music by Joan Lowrance - 8/1/18

G   B   D+ E+ C+   G   D   E   C
"Give" ear O <u>heavens</u> and I will speak:

G   B   D+ C+   A   B   G   E   C
And hear, <u>O earth</u>, the words of my mouth. .

C   E   G   E   D   E   C
Let my <u>teaching</u> drop as rain,

G   B   D+ C+ B   G   E
My speech <u>distill</u>   as the <u>dew</u>,

G   B   A   F   D   F   E   C
As raindrops on the <u>tender herb</u>,

E   G   B   A   F   D   C
And as showers on the grass.

C   E   G   E   G   B   A   B   G
For I proclaim the <u>name</u> of the <u>Lord</u>:

C E   G   B   D+ E+   C+
<u>Ascribe greatness</u> to <u>our God</u>.

Chorus:

C E G B   A   B G A F
He is the Rock, His work is perfect;

 C E G B   A B G
For all His ways are justice,

D F A C+ B C+ A   B A G   C   E   G B A B C+ (slowly
A God of truth and without injustice; Righteous and upright is He.   repeat
line)

Our Father Gives Good Things

Matthew 7:7-8

Song & Music by Joan Lowrance - 3/16/18

```
C    E  G  F  A   BA  B  G
```
Ask, and it will be given to you;

```
 C    E   G   A  F
```
Seek, and you will find;

```
 C    E  G  A  G   A  F   G  E
```
Knock, and it will be opened to you.

Chorus:

```
C   E   G E   G  B  C+  D+ C+   A    F    G   E   F
```
For your Father who is in heaven gives good things to those

```
 D    A   D   B   E   D    C+
```
who ask, who seek, and who knock. (end in middle C)

Verse 2:

```
 C   E G   F   G    A     B G
```
For every one who asks receives;

```
 E    C    E    G     F
```
and he who seeks, finds;

```
 C    E   G   F   A
```
and to him who knocks,

```
 G   A  G   B  G
```
it will be opened.

20

Our Father

Matthew 6:9-13

Song & Music by Joan Lowrance - 2/16/07

E   C D C -A C E D

Our Father who art in <u>heaven</u>,

C -A   D -B   C

hallow be thy <u>name</u>.

C -A D   C

Thy kingdom <u>come</u>,

C -A D   C C -A C -G

Thy will be <u>done</u> in <u>me</u> on <u>earth</u>

C -A -G -B D C

as it is in <u>heaven</u>.

C -A D   C C -A -G C

Give us this <u>day</u> our daily bread

C -G -A -B D E C   C

and forgive us our <u>trespasses</u>

D -B -G -B D   E C C

as we forgive our <u>trespassers</u>.

C -A -G -B DE G   A G

And lead us not into <u>temptation</u>

C -A -G -B D F   E C

and deliver us <u>from</u> evil,

```
 C   F   A C+  C+  A
```
for <u>thine</u> is the <u>kingdom</u>

```
 G   C+  F+ E+   G  C+  F+E+  C+F+E+
```
and the <u>power</u> and the <u>glory</u>   <u>forever</u>

```
D+   F+E+   C+
```
<u>and ever more</u>.

```
C+E+G+F+   CEGC
```
<u>Amen</u>,   <u>Amen</u>.

Tithings and Offerings

1 Chronicles 29:10-14

Song & Music by Joan Lowrance - 3/5/19

Chorus:

   B A   B   G   B   D+ D+ C+A
Blessed are <u>You</u>, Lord God of <u>Israel</u>,

 G   B A   B D+ C+ B   D+C+
our Father, <u>forever and ever</u>.

  G C+ B A B   D+ B   G C+ B   A   B   C+
For all that is in <u>heaven</u> and in the <u>earth</u> is <u>Yours</u>.

Verse 1:

   B G A   B D+ E+ C+
<u>Yours</u> is the kingdom, <u>O Lord</u>,

  B   G   G C+B A   B   D+   D+ E+ C+
and You are <u>exalted</u> as head over all.

   B   A B   B   C+B   B   B   G
Both riches and honor come from <u>You</u>,

   G   C+   B   AB C+
<u>And You reign over all</u>. (2)

Chorus:

   B A   B   G   B   D+ D+ C+A
Blessed are <u>You</u>, Lord God of <u>Israel</u>,

G   B A   B D+ C+ B D+C+
<u>our Father, forever and ever</u>.

 G C+ B A B D+ B G C+ B A   B C+
For all that is in <u>heaven</u> and in the <u>earth</u> is <u>Yours</u>.

Verse 2:

 B   G A   B G
<u>Now</u> therefore, our God,

C+   B   G
<u>We</u> thank you

C+   G   B D+E+D+ C+
And praise <u>Your glorious name</u>.

 G E C D G E C D E C
But <u>who</u> am I, and <u>who</u> are my people,

 C   E   G   B A B G BA B
That we should be able to offer so

 G B D+ E+ C+
<u>willingly</u> as this?

 C E G   B   A G
For all things come <u>from You</u>,

 C E G B A G BA   G
And of Your <u>own</u> we have <u>given You</u>.

24

Chorus:

  B A   B G   B   D+ D+ C+A
Blessed are <u>You</u>, Lord God of <u>Israel</u>,

  G   B A   B D+ C+ B D+C+
<u>our Father, forever and ever</u>.

  G C+ B A B D+ B   G C+B   A   B C+
For all that is in <u>heaven</u> and in the <u>earth</u> is <u>Yours</u>.

C+E+G+F+   C E G C
 <u>Amen</u>,   <u>Amen</u>.

Hello, Lord

Song and Music by Mark Kovach - 2/9/15

Wide Honky Tonk
Moderately slow

 G C   E
Hello, Lord,

C   -A   C D   C   D   E   D C
It's been awhile, but now I'm ready.

-A   C   D   E   D   C
I want'a walk with You.

-A   C   D   E   D   C
I want'a talk with You,

-A   C   D   E   C+ A   G   A   F
I want'a sing praises to the Lord.

-A   C   E   D   F   E   D   C
I want'a be guided by You.

-A   CD   E   F   E   C
I want'a be just like You.

-A   C   D   E   C+ A   G   A   F
I want'a sing praises to the Lord.

-A   C   D   E   C+A G A   C+A G A
I want'a sing Hallelujah, Hallelujah,

C +A G A   G   A   F
Hallelujah to the Lord.

26

C+ G A G A F
Sing praises to the Lord.

-A C D E D F C
I want'a be loved by You

C -A C D E C
the way that I love You.

-A C D E C+ A G A F
I want'a sing praises to the Lord.

-A C D E D C
I want'a worship You,

-A C D E D G C
I want'a glorify You.

-A C D E C+ A G A F
I want'a sing praises to the Lord.

-A C D E C+ A G A C+ A G A
I want'a sing Hallelujah, Hallelujah,

C+ A G A G A F
Hallelujah to the Lord.

C+ G A G A F
Sing praises to the Lord.

C+ G A G A F
Sing praises to the Lord.

Oh, My Jesus

Song & Music by Joan Lowrance - 6/12/14

(Slowly)

 E   D   C C
Oh my Jesus,

 E -B C   C
How I love Thee.

 C   E   G   C+   A   B   G
Oh, to love You more each day.

  E   -B   C E D
What more can I say?

 D -B   C   E   G   B A
You are my hope and promise

E G   C+   B   A D+ C+
to be with You forever.

 E   G   B   A   A C+ B A C+ B   G
For You shall reign forever and ever more

 G   E   G   B   A   C+
and we shall give You praise (Repeat for ending)

 A   B   G A   C+
for all of our days

28

```
A   G    C+    A    G G              C C
in Your house, dear Jesus. (2nd time - Jesus)


C+ E+ G+   F+          C E G   C
    A      men,          A    men
```

I Will Visit You

Jeremiah 29:10-14

Song & Music by Joan Lowrance - 10/3/16

C E G A F   C E G   B   A   F   A   F
I will visit <u>you</u> and perform <u>My good</u> word <u>toward you</u>,

E   D   E F E D   E   D   C
and cause you to return to this <u>place</u>.

C   E   G   B   G   C   E   G   B   G   A   F   D
For I <u>know</u> the <u>thoughts</u> that I think <u>toward you</u>, <u>says the Lord</u>,

F   G   E   E   D   E F D
thoughts of <u>peace</u> and not of evil,

C   G   E   D   A F G B   G
to give you a <u>future and a hope</u>.

Chorus:

C E GA F
I will visit <u>you</u>,

C E GA B G
I will listen to <u>you</u>,

C   E G F   D   E C
and I will be <u>found by you</u>.   (repeat ending slowly the 2nd time)

Verse 2

C   E G A GB G C E G   A B G
Then you will call upon <u>Me</u> and go and <u>pray to Me</u>,

C E G AG A F   A   F   D
and I will <u>listen to you</u>, <u>says the Lord</u>.

E   D E F   D   F   G E
And you will seek Me and <u>find Me</u>,

C   E   G   A F E D   E   C
when you search <u>for Me</u> <u>with all your heart</u>,

C E G   F   E C   A   F   D
I will be <u>found by you</u>, <u>says the Lord</u>.

Are You Jim

Lyrics By Jim Morris
Music By Joan Lowrance – 09/03

C   E   G C+ E+ D+   B
There was a time when I searched

C+ D+ C+ B   G   D   C
for a smile and found no one.

E   G   B   E+ C+   B   G
Then you came <u>along</u> and said,

C E   C
Are you Jim?

E   G   D F#   G   A G   (The Black Key on right of F key)
Then with your smile and <u>splendor</u>,

E   C   D F# G
my heart was <u>captured</u>,

B   D+   E+ D+ C+
my soul <u>surrendered</u>,

G F# G D
I was in love.

E C E G D   C   E F# G
Now, I no <u>longer</u> search for a smile,

B D+   B   G F# G D
for you have <u>given</u> me yours

C   E   G   C+   E+ D+
where it grows day by day,

B C+ B   G   D
<u>showered</u> by your love.

```
C  E  G  C+ D+  C+  B G   D
I  trust in  it  and  I  treasure it
```

```
C  D E   C  C   E F#  G
and I keep it close to my heart.
```

```
G  C  D  F#  G  D   C
Today is your birthday and
```

```
E G   C+ E+ D+ E+  C+ A   G
I give you my gift with all my love,
```

```
C  E  G  C  E  G   C
a smile for you from my heart.
```

```
    D    E    C
Signed love, Jim.
```

(This is Jim's love song to his wife, Darlene, on her birthday.)

Go to Joan's Women's Bible Study at joanswomensbiblestudy.com and read Jim and Darlene's love story that is debuted in the Women's Bible Study under "The Women's Role" and also under other Family Topics in "Your Dream Home 1.4" which speaks about the great business and home insurance policy they have to offer at very reasonable prices which few people can beat.

www.ingramcontent.com/pod-product-compliance
Lightning Source LLC
LaVergne TN
LVHW081322060426
835509LV00015B/1646